TRAVEL DIARY
—— O F   T H E ——

HOLY LAND

JOHN BIMSON

With the Compliments of Heavenly International Tours Inc.
Milwaukee, Wisconsin, USA
(800) 322-8622

A LION BOOK

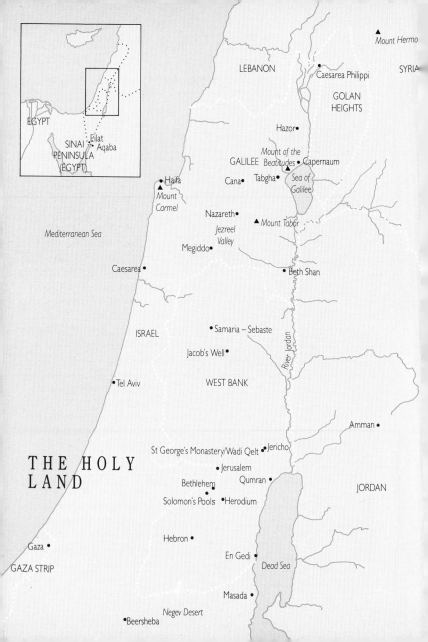

THE HOLY LAND

This full colour companion-guide is designed specially for your holiday of a lifetime. Plenty of space is left for you to write your own impressions, making this a personal memento to treasure long after your holiday has ended.

CONTENTS

The Holy Land: Its Geography and Climate 4
A Brief History of the Land and its Peoples 5

Jerusalem: Damascus Gate 14
Jerusalem: Via Dolorosa 16
Jerusalem: Holy Sepulchre 18
Jerusalem: Western Wall 24
Jericho 26
River Jordan 28
Wadi Qelt: St George's Monastery 32
Qumran 34
En Gedi 36
Masada 38
Bethlehem 42
Solomon's Pools 44
Herodium. 46
Hebron 48

Beersheba 50
Jacob's Well 52
Samaria-Sebaste 54
Beth Shan 58
Caesarea 60
Mount Carmel 62
Jezreel Valley 64
Megiddo 66
Mount Tabor 68
Nazareth 70
Sea of Galilee 72
Capernaum 74
Tabgha (Heptapegon) 76
Mount of the Beatitudes 78
Hazor 80
Caesarea Philippi (Banyas) 82
Mount Hermon 84

General Information 86
Peoples and Faiths 90

THE HOLY LAND
ITS GEOGRAPHY AND CLIMATE

For a relatively small area, the Holy Land contains some surprising contrasts. In the north the peaks of Mount Hermon rise to 3,030m/9,232ft and are never free from snow; a mere 185km/125 miles to the south, the shore of the Dead Sea is 400m/1,290ft below sea-level, and there the daytime temperature in summer may reach a baking 40°C (104°F). A traveller crossing the country from west to east would also encounter some striking changes within a short distance. At the latitude of Jerusalem it is only 55km/36 miles from the coast to where the central hills reach their highest altitude (1,000m/3,280ft), and only another 36km/24 miles from there to the bottom of the deep rift-valley where the Jordan enters the Dead Sea.

The central hills run the length of the country, interrupted by the broad valley of Jezreel. In ancient times they were well wooded. Their deforestation was a long process, already underway in Old Testament times. The agricultural terraces which now characterize the hills were developed as the forests were cleared, and would have been a common sight in the biblical period, though on a smaller scale than today.

In many places, soil-erosion has greatly impoverished the land since Bible times. Visitors should remember that hillsides which today are bare rock were once places where crops grew or evergreen oaks spread their shade. In some parts of the country, modern tree-planting helps us to envisage what large areas must have looked like in the biblical period. Until clearance of the hills for farming began, about two centuries before David, most settlements were on the fringes of the hills, along the coastal plain and in the Jordan valley.

An understanding of the Holy Land is helped by an appreciation of its wider setting. With the Mediterranean to the west and the Syrian desert to the east, it has always been important as a bridge connecting Africa (primarily Egypt) in the south with Asia in the north. This is why it was so often fought over during the biblical period. The Bible mentions two routes of international importance which passed through the land: 'the way of the sea' which ran along the coastal plain, connecting Egypt with Syria and north-west Mesopotamia, and 'the King's Highway' which ran north through the Transjordanian highlands to Damascus.

Most pilgrims and tourists make short visits to the Holy Land in spring or summer, and so never experience the contrasting seasons of the area. The spring sees the start of the dry season, the last of the rains usually falling in April. In the Bible, harvest-time does not mean late summer and autumn but spring (April–May). That was when the barley and wheat were harvested; during the summer, fruits were gathered.

The glorious flowers which cover the hillsides in spring are soon gone, and the long summer drought sees many areas turn from a lush green to a parched brown. An experience of the heat of such a summer helps us to appreciate why the Bible uses water as a symbol of God's presence and blessing. There is usually little or no rain until October. In December, January and February the rains are heavy. These are also the coldest months, and the rain can fall as snow in the hills. Jerusalem's average annual rainfall is actually about the same as London's, but it receives almost all of it in fifty days during winter. (For a table of temperatures, see the Information pages at the back.)

A BRIEF HISTORY
OF THE LAND AND ITS PEOPLES

A visitor to the Holy Land will see evidence of a rich variety of cultures, some ancient and vanished, some still very much alive. The cultures and faiths represented there, by archaeological remains, ancient and modern buildings and living communities, have their origins in a long and complex history. The following outline is intended to help the visitor understand that history.

THE BIBLICAL PERIOD FROM ABRAHAM TO SAUL

The Holy Land enters the long sweep of biblical history soon after 2000BC. That was roughly when Abraham journeyed from Mesopotamia to Canaan, in response to God's call and promise. In the time of Abraham's grandson, Jacob, his descendants left Canaan to avoid famine and settled in Egypt. During the next four centuries the growing Hebrew nation was pressed into slavery by the Egyptians, eventually escaping under the leadership of Moses. Biblical scholars disagree over the date of this event; some place it around 1450BC, while many prefer a date two centuries later, around 1250BC.

THE LAND
OF THE OLD
TESTAMENT

- Sidon
  LEBANON
  Damascus
- Zarephath
  SYRIA
  ▲ Mt Hermon
  AR
- Tyre
  - Dan
  PHOENICIA
  - Hazor
  Lake of
  Chinnereth
  BASHAN
  ▲ Mt Carmel
  ▲ Mt Tabor
  - Endor
  - Shunem
  Megiddo
  Valley of Jezreel
  Ramoth-gilead
  - Beth-shan
  The Great Sea
  ▲ Mt Gilboa ▲
  - Dothan
  - Jabesh-gilead
  ISRAEL
  GILEAD
  Plain of
  Sharon
  Samaria
  - Tirzah
  ▲ Mt Ebal
  Penuel
  ▲ Mt Gerizim
  - Shechem
  Succoth
  - River Jabbok
  Mahanaim
  - Joppa
  - Shiloh
  AMMON
  Mizpah
  Bethel
  Michmash
  - Ai
  - Rabbah
  Gibeon
  - Gilgal
  Kiriath-jearim
  - Gibeah
  Jericho
  - Shittim
  Ekron
  - Jerusalem
  - Beth-shemesh
  Ashdod
  Makkedah
  - Bethlehem
  ▲ Mt Nebo
  Ashkelon
  Libnah
  - Lachish
  - Mamre
  Gaza
  Hebron
  Salt
  Sea
  PHILISTIA
  JUDAH
  - Engedi
  - Gath
  - Ziklag
  River Arnon
  MOAB
  - Ar
  - Beersheba

River Jordan

Arabah Valley

After forty years spent in the wilderness to the south of Canaan, the Israelites moved north through Transjordan where some of them conquered territory. After crossing the Jordan the tribes embarked on a conquest of Canaan, led by Joshua. Their successes were mostly in the hills, leaving pockets of Canaanite resistance in the lowlands. In the centuries which followed, during the time of the Judges, these became a serious threat, because Canaanite culture and religion were absorbed into Israelite society, destroying its cohesion. The tribes then became easy prey for invaders and oppressors. The danger posed by the Philistines was particularly acute, and this led to the demand for a king who would lead the tribes in united military action. The prophet Samuel anointed Saul as Israel's first king around 1030BC.

THE UNITED MONARCHY

Under Saul the nation's institutions changed very little, but his successor, David, transformed a loose confederation of tribes into a nation with a single capital at Jerusalem and a small empire of subject states. David's impressive military achievements left his son Solomon in a powerful position. He was able to engage in international trading enterprises which vastly increased the nation's prosperity. The temple which he built in Jerusalem was lavishly adorned with gold.

However, wealth was concentrated in the capital and the administrative centres, and many of Solomon's ordinary subjects felt exploited. They were burdened by heavy taxation and a forced labour scheme which Solomon introduced to further his ambitious building projects. Most of this burden seems to have fallen on the ten northern tribes, and around 930BC they broke away to form a separate kingdom under Jeroboam I. This was at the beginning of the reign of Solomon's son and successor, Rehoboam, who continued to rule the southern tribes of Judah and Benjamin.

THE TWO KINGDOMS

For the next two centuries two kingdoms existed side by side: Israel in the north and Judah in the south. While Judah continued to be ruled from Jerusalem by descendants of David, Israel had a succession of royal houses and capitals. Around 876BC Omri moved the capital to Samaria, and there it remained for the rest of the northern kingdom's history.

Israel was repeatedly threatened by armies from the north, from Aram and Assyria. From 745BC Assyria became the dominant power of the ancient world, and soon both Israel and Judah were her vassals. In 722BC Israel rebelled against Assyria; Samaria was destroyed by Assyrian armies and many of her people were deported. The prophets Amos and Hosea had predicted this catastrophe as a punishment for Israel's persistent idolatry and deep-rooted social injustice.

From that time onwards Judah was alone, with an Assyrian province on her northern border. Around 630BC Assyria's empire began to crumble, and Judah briefly enjoyed independence under Josiah. However, battles between Egypt and Babylon over the control of Syria and Palestine resulted in Babylon becoming the new super-power of the region under Nebuchadrezzar. From 605BC Judah was his vassal. Through the folly of her later kings, Judah followed Israel along the road to disaster, in spite of the warnings of the prophet Jeremiah. A rebellion against Babylon by Jehoiakim resulted in the cream of the population being deported to Babylon in 597BC, and a rebellion by Zedekiah resulted in a further deportation and the destruction of Jerusalem in 587BC.

EXILE AND RESTORATION

When the northern tribes were exiled by the Assyrians in 722BC, they were dispersed and eventually lost their national identity. Fortunately, Judah fared somewhat better during her exile in Babylon. The Judean exiles were settled in communities where their national and religious identity was kept alive.

In 539BC, almost fifty years after the destruction of Jerusalem, Babylon fell to Cyrus, king of Persia, and the Babylonian realms, including Palestine, became part of a vast Persian empire. Cyrus sponsored the restoration of local temples for the worship of the gods of his subject peoples and, as part of this policy, the exiled Judeans were allowed to return home to rebuild the temple in Jerusalem.

The first wave of people returning reached Judah in 537BC, but within a few years the rebuilding project had lost impetus. In 520BC, fresh inspiration was provided by the prophets Haggai and Zechariah, and in 516BC the new temple was completed.

In the middle of the next century, under the leadership of Ezra, a second group of exiles returned, and soon after, Nehemiah was appointed governor of Judah by the Persians. Between them, Ezra and Nehemiah gave Judaism the form in which it was to survive through the following centuries.

It is important to appreciate that after the exile the Jews were no longer a nation defined by geography. Although many exiles had returned from Babylon, many more remained there, having thoroughly adapted to life away from their homeland. By the close of the Old Testament period, around 400BC, there were Jewish communities not only in Babylon, but throughout the Persian empire, from Egypt to what is now eastern Iran.

THE COMING OF THE GREEKS

Judah remained part of Persia's empire until 333BC, when the Persian realms were conquered by Alexander of Macedon (the Great). Alexander began a policy of hellenization—the promotion of Greek culture— throughout his massive empire. When he died in 323BC, his empire was divided among his generals, who continued the hellenization process. Palestine initially belonged to Ptolemy, whose dynasty ruled Egypt, but in 198BC it was taken from the Ptolemies by the dynasty of Seleucus, which ruled Syria and Mesopotamia.

Some Jews in Jerusalem were strongly opposed to the hellenization of their culture, as it was beginning to threaten the distinctiveness of Judaism. In 167BC the Seleucid king, Antiochus IV, fearful for the stability of his southern realm, introduced measures to eradicate Judaism completely from its homeland. But the Jews rebelled under the leadership of Judas Maccabeus, and in 164BC Antiochus revoked his anti-Jewish decrees.

The successors of Judas Maccabeus went on to fight for political as well as religious freedom. In 128BC this was achieved, and the Hasmonean priest-kings ruled an independent Judean kingdom for the next sixty-five years.

THE ROMAN PERIOD (63BC–AD324)

As the Seleucid empire disintegrated, the Roman general Pompey invaded Syria to bring stability to the region. He also intervened in Judean affairs to end a civil war which had broken out between rival factions of the Hasmonean house. As a result Judah (now Judea) became tributary to Rome in 63BC. From 37–4BC Herod the Great ruled Judea as a client-king of Rome.

Jesus of Nazareth was born in Bethlehem in the last years of Herod's reign. Soon after Herod's death, Judea was brought back under Rome's direct control and was governed by procurators. It was one of these procurators, Pontius Pilate, who authorized Jesus' crucifixion around AD30.

Although the ministry of Jesus was to have a world-wide impact, at the time it was but one small ingredient in a turbulent century. In AD66 Jewish discontent with a succession of Roman procurators boiled over and became an open rebellion. The Romans crushed it violently, and in AD70 Jerusalem and its temple were destroyed. The temple was never rebuilt, and the event was a watershed for Judaism, which had to function thereafter without temple worship and sacrifices. A second Jewish revolt in AD132–35 was also crushed, and the emperor Hadrian rebuilt Jerusalem as a Roman city from which Jews were excluded. The focus of Jewish life shifted to Galilee.

THE BYZANTINE PERIOD (AD324–640)

For almost three centuries Christianity spread through the Roman empire as an underground movement. Christians were treated with suspicion and sometimes persecuted. Then in AD313 the emperor Constantine, who ruled the western half of a divided empire, decreed that all religions would be equally tolerated. After AD324, when he gained control of the eastern part of the empire as well, he made Christianity the official religion of his whole realm. Constantine moved his capital from Rome to Byzantium, which he renamed Constantinople.

Constantine's policy had a dramatic effect on life in the Holy Land. Sites associated with Jesus' ministry, death, resurrection and ascension were adorned with churches, and pilgrims flocked to them. The Christian population increased, and Jerusalem prospered once again.

THE EARLY ARAB AND CRUSADER PERIODS (AD640–1291)

In the seventh century, inspired by the new faith of Islam, Arab armies swept northwards. The Byzantine empire was by then too weak to offer resistance. Jerusalem fell to the caliph Omar in AD637. A succession of caliphs ruled the Holy Land from various capitals for the next four centuries, during which Christian pilgrimages were tolerated. This changed

PLACES OF THE GOSPELS

ITUREA

SYRIA

• Caesarea Philippi

TETRARCHY OF PHILIP

• Ptolemais

Chorazin •
Capernaum • • Bethsaida
Gennesaret •
Lake Galilee
Cana •
Tiberias •

GALILEE

Nazareth •

• Nain

• Gadara

DECAPOLIS

Mediterranean Sea

• Caesarea

Salim • Aenon

• Sychar

SAMARIA

• Antipatris

• Joppa

River Jordan

• Lydda

PEREA

Jericho •

Emmaus •
Jerusalem • • Bethphage
JUDEA • Bethany
Bethlehem •

Dead Sea

IDUMEA

NABATEAN KINGDOM

in 1077 when Seljuk Turks from central Asia took the Holy Land from the Fatimid caliphs who were ruling it from Cairo. Christian pilgrims were molested and so pilgrimages ceased.

This prompted the First Crusade (1097–99), which was an attempt to regain the holy places. Although Jerusalem was back in the hands of the Fatimid caliphs by 1099, the religious fervour of the Crusade made it unstoppable. Its success resulted in the creation of the Latin Kingdom of Jerusalem, which lasted until 1187. Tragically, the Crusade was marked by bloody excesses against the Muslims of the Holy Land, and this provoked an equal inflexibility on the part of Islam.

In 1187 the Crusaders were decisively defeated by Saladin and their Kingdom of Jerusalem was never restored, in spite of six further Crusades. However, they maintained a presence in the Holy Land for another century. In 1250 Saladin's dynasty, the Ayyubids, were replaced in Egypt by the Mamelukes, who embarked on the systematic expulsion of the Crusaders from the Holy Land. This was completed in 1291 with the fall of Acre.

THE MAMELUKE AND OTTOMAN PERIODS (1291–1918)

Under its harsh Mameluke rulers Palestine became something of a political and cultural backwater, though there were visits by pilgrims and scholars from Europe.

In 1453 the Ottoman Turks captured Constantinople. Under its new name, Istanbul, it became the capital of their growing empire. They defeated the Mamelukes in 1516 and by the next year Egypt and the Holy Land were in their hands. The reign of Suleiman the Magnificent (1520–66) was the high point of the Ottoman empire's history, when it reached from Vienna to the south-eastern tip of the Arabian peninsula. Suleiman built the walls which still surround the Old City of Jerusalem today.

Soon after Suleiman's reign the empire went into three centuries of decline. Palestine was neglected and its population dwindled. However, the Jewish community grew as Jews fleeing from persecutions in Russia settled there.

In the First World War the Turks were allied with Germany, and after their defeat the League of Nations divided the remnants of the old Ottoman empire into mandate territories. The Holy Land, along with

Mesopotamia, was given to Britain. The territory west of the Jordan was designated 'Palestine'.

MODERN DEVELOPMENTS

In the Balfour Declaration of 1917 Britain stated that it favoured the creation of a Jewish state in Palestine. Not surprisingly, Jewish immigration to the Holy Land rose sharply under the British mandate. From the 1930s, Hitler's attempted extermination of Jews in Europe (the Holocaust) increased it further. Tensions rose between the Jewish community, which was hoping for the creation of its own state, and the Arab population for which the Holy Land had been home for centuries.

By 1947 the Jewish population of the Holy Land had reached 650,000 —one-third of the total. In that year, in response to escalating violence between the Jewish and Arab communities, the United Nations passed a resolution favouring the creation of a Jewish state. In 1948 Britain terminated its mandate government and withdrew, and the state of Israel came into existence.

Immediately, war broke out between the new state and Arab nations opposed to its creation. This was the first Arab-Israeli war. It was ended by armistice agreements in 1949. However, in 1956 it was followed by a second war (the Suez incident), and in 1967 by a third (the 'Six Day War'). This ended with Israel taking the Sinai and the Gaza Strip from Egypt, the Golan Heights from Syria, and a part of the central hill country, known as the West Bank, from Jordan. The latter had included the Old City of Jerusalem, so its capture resulted in Jerusalem's reunification. A fourth Arab-Israeli war occurred in 1973 (the 'Yom Kippur War').

By the Camp David Accord of 1980, the Sinai (excluding the Gaza Strip) was returned to Egypt. The other regions taken in 1967 (known as the occupied territories) are still under Israeli military control. Their populations are largely Arab and include many Palestinians who fled to those territories as refugees when Israel was established. Today opinion is divided between the belief (perhaps held by most of the international community) that no just peace is possible until the occupied territories are back in Arab hands, and Israel's view that national security depends on her continuing to occupy them. The interested visitor should try to understand both sides of the argument over this very sensitive issue.

The Damascus Gate has for centuries been the main entry and exit on the north side of Jerusalem. The present gate was built in 1537, but there has been a gate here since the first century AD. One of the three arches of this earliest gate can still be seen below the present gate on its east side. It now gives public access to excavated parts of the gate-tower.

The first-century gate was built by Herod Agrippa (AD41–44). Ten years earlier, at the time of Jesus' crucifixion, the northern limit of Jerusalem lay further south. Herod's attack on Christians in Jerusalem and his sudden death in Caesarea are recorded in Acts 12.

'King Herod arrested some who belonged to the church, intending to persecute them. He had James . . . put to death with the sword.' Acts 12:1–2

The exterior of the Damascus Gate. Part of
Agrippa's gate can be seen below and to
the left, indicating the lower ground-level of
New Testament times.

JERUSALEM VIA DOLOROSA

Although Holy Week processions took place in Jerusalem as early as the fourth century AD, these did not follow the present Via Dolorosa ('Way of Sorrow') and did not involve the Stations of the Cross. The traditional fourteen Stations of the Cross evolved as a devotional practice in Europe from about AD 1400 onwards. In the following centuries, through the visits of European pilgrims, they acquired locations in Jerusalem. Five Stations of the Cross were located within the Church of the Holy Sepulchre, and the rest were strung out along what is now the Via Dolorosa. The present route was not settled on until the eighteenth century, and there is little chance that it relates to historical fact.

Here is the beginning of the Via Dolorosa, looking west under the arch known as the 'Ecce Homo' (Latin for 'Behold the man') because of Pilate's words in John 19:5. The arch actually dates from either AD 41 or 135, and so was not standing in Jesus' day.

It was at the praetorium, the Jerusalem residence of the Roman governor, that Pilate reluctantly sentenced Jesus to death. From there Jesus, already weakened by a scourging, was led out through a gate of the city to the place of execution. Although traditionally located where the Via Dolorosa now begins, the praetorium is more likely to have stood near the present Citadel. However, the value of the Via Dolorosa lies in the events it calls to mind, not in its location.

'As they led him away, they seized Simon from Cyrene. . . and put the cross on him and made him carry it behind Jesus. A large number of people followed him. . . . Two other men, both criminals, were also led out with him to be executed. When they came to the place called the Skull, there they crucified him. . .' Luke 23:26–27, 32–33

The Church of the Holy Sepulchre is an unappealing structure shared by six denominations. Most of the present exterior dates from 1810 (following a fire in 1808), but the building incorporates many eleventh to twelfth century elements, and parts of the church built by Constantine in AD326–335 are also preserved.

Since at least the fourth century AD, and perhaps much earlier, this has been revered as the spot where Jesus' ministry culminated in his crucifixion, burial and resurrection. The outcrop of rock identified as Golgotha, and the traditional catacomb of Joseph of Arimathea, are both incorporated in the extensive building.

'. . . You are looking for Jesus, who was crucified. He is not here; he has risen, just as he said. Come and see the place where he lay.' Matthew 28:5–6

Now set in a cramped part of the walled city, the site of the church lay outside the walls of Jesus' day and there were certainly Jewish burials in the area. There is therefore a good chance that it correctly preserves the location of the crucifixion and resurrection.

This area, originally a rocky plateau, lay immediately north of the city of David's time. Its height and exposure to the wind made it an excellent threshing-floor. David bought it from Araunah the Jebusite in order to build an altar there, and in Solomon's reign (about 970–930BC) it became the site of the temple. Solomon's temple was destroyed by the Babylonians in 587BC, but the second temple, built after the Jews returned from exile, stood on the same site. The second temple was completed by Zerubbabel in 516BC. It underwent a number of changes during the next five centuries, but the most dramatic was its complete reconstruction by Herod the Great. Herod expanded the hilltop by creating a massive rectangular platform, roughly 480×300m/ 1,560×975ft, to support the temple courts. The huge retaining walls which Herod built on the west, south and east sides are what define the temple mount today. The vast undertaking was begun around 20–19BC. Although the new structure was dedicated in 10BC, work was still going on at the time of Jesus' ministry (John 2:20) and the temple did not receive its finishing touches until AD63 —only seven years before the Romans destroyed it! For much of the six centuries following the Roman destruction, Herod's vast enclosure was abandoned (it was used as a rubbish dump by Byzantine Christians). Then, following the Muslim conquest, the Umayyad caliphs undertook to beautify it again. The Dome of the Rock (not a mosque but a shrine) was built around AD690, and the el-Aksa mosque about twenty years later. The name given to the temple mount by Muslims—Haram esh-Sharif—means 'The Noble Sanctuary', a title justified by the tranquillity and spaciousness which characterize it.

The Dome of the Rock is seen here across the Kidron Valley from the Mount of Olives. Beneath the sealed Golden Gate, to the right of the picture, the remains of an earlier gate lie buried; Jesus probably used this gate when he entered the temple area from the Mount of Olives.

The temple built by Solomon is described in great detail in 1 Kings chapters 6 and 7. The Bible contains no equivalent description of the temple which Zerubbabel built to replace it, but it was evidently inferior to the original. However, Herod's temple, with its expansive courts, columned porticoes and fine masonry, outshone even Solomon's. This was the temple Jesus knew. In Luke chapter 2 we read that he was taken there by Joseph and Mary as a child, and as a man he attended its festivals and taught in its courts.

In the eastern portico, known as Solomon's, Jesus was accused of blasphemy by his audience and narrowly avoided arrest and stoning. In the portico which ran along the southern side, money changers and various dealers were allowed to set up their stalls. Jesus' attack on this practice increased popular support for him and strengthened the authorities' resolve to put him to death.

This is an aerial view of Herod's temple platform, looking north. In its original grandeur it dominated the city of New Testament times. Today the Dome of the Rock stands on or near the site of the temple itself. To the right the Kidron Valley runs below the eastern wall of the enclosure.

'On reaching Jerusalem, Jesus entered the temple area and began driving out those who were buying and selling there. He overturned the tables of the money changers and the benches of those selling doves. . . And as he taught them, he said, "Is it not written: 'My house will be called a house of prayer for all nations'? But you have made it 'a den of robbers'." The chief priests and the teachers of the law heard this and began looking for a way to kill him, for they feared him. . .' Mark 11:15, 17–18

Houses of the old Jewish Quarter once extended to within a few metres of the western wall, part of Herod's temple enclosure. After the reunification of Jerusalem in 1967, these houses were removed to create the spacious plaza which serves as a Jewish place of prayer. South of the ramp to the present Moors' Gate, archaeologists have uncovered many structures from Herod's time onwards.

The prayer area lies in front of the western wall. The first seven courses of large stones above the modern pavement belong to Herod's temple enclosure. The smaller stones above these are Muslim and Crusader repair work. Herod's masonry extends 5m/16ft below the plaza to the pavement of Jesus' time.

The large and finely-cut blocks of masonry in the walls of the temple enclosure drew expressions of awe and admiration from Jesus' disciples. However, Jesus prophesied that the whole edifice would be destroyed—a prediction fulfilled by the armies of Titus in AD 70. (It became traditional for Jews to visit the western wall to mourn this destruction; hence the name 'Wailing Wall' by which it was commonly known before 1967.)

'As he was leaving the temple, one of his disciples said to him, "Look, Teacher! What massive stones! What magnificent buildings!" "Do you see all these great buildings?" replied Jesus. "Not one stone here will be left on another; every one will be thrown down".'
Mark 13:1–2

JERICHO

In the Jordan valley about 13km/8 miles north of the Dead Sea lies the fertile oasis of Jericho, fed by an abundant spring. The oasis attracted a settlement as early as 9000BC, and by 7500BC this had become a walled town—one of the oldest in the world. It is also the lowest, 258m/840ft below sea-level! To the west, where the central hills begin to rise up from the plain, stands the Mount of Temptation, traditionally associated with Matthew 4:8–10.

Best known as the first Canaanite city taken by Joshua's troops, Jericho was rebuilt under the Israelite monarchy and features in one of the stories of Elisha. Hence the spring is today called 'Elisha's Spring'. New Testament Jericho lay further south, at the end of the Wadi Qelt (see page 32).

'When the trumpets sounded, the people shouted, and. . . when the people gave a loud shout, the wall collapsed; so every man charged straight in, and they took the city.' Joshua 6:20

The ruin-mound of Old Testament Jericho is seen here from the air, looking towards the north-east. Because of the many palm trees growing in this verdant spot, Jericho was also known as 'the city of palms'.

The Jordan follows a sinuous course
through its flood-plain, meandering so
wildly that its actual length is more than
twice the distance between the meeting of
its headwaters and the Dead Sea. In Old
Testament times the thick vegetation
bordering the river was the haunt of lions.
Jeremiah 49:19

Fed by several springs at the foot of Mount Hermon, the Jordan flows in the northern part of a great rift-valley which extends through the Gulf of Aqaba and down to the great lakes of East Africa. The Jordan ('Descender') is aptly named. The point where its headwaters meet is 70m/230ft above sea-level; a mere 120km/ 75 miles to the south, where the river enters the Dead Sea, it is 400m/1,290ft *below* sea-level. The shore of the Dead Sea is the lowest dry land on the earth's surface. The high temperatures here produce a rapid rate of evaporation, and as a result there is no outflow south of the Dead Sea. The Jordan is too shallow to be navigable, its depth ranging between 1 and 3m/3 and 10ft. There were no bridges in biblical times, but the river is never more than 30m/100ft wide and there were fords at the shallower places.

Although the tribes of Reuben, Gad and Manasseh possessed territory east of the Jordan, the river was generally considered to be Israel's eastern boundary. Hence the crossing of the Jordan under Joshua's leadership marked Israel's entry into her promised land. The crossing took place from Shittim in the plains of Moab, roughly opposite Jericho. The river was in flood at the time because it was spring, when the melting snows on the lower slopes of Hermon swell its sources. However, the Israelites were able to cross because the waters were temporarily cut off some way upstream.

John the Baptist carried on his ministry around the Jordan, and it was in the Jordan that he baptized Jesus. Although this event took place somewhere on the eastern side of the river, it has traditionally been commemorated at el-Maghtas, on the west bank 9km/5.5 miles south-east of Jericho. By his baptism Jesus identified himself with those being baptized as a sign of repentance, and also committed himself to his mission. His baptism was followed by the temptations; the traditional Mount of Temptation, Jebel Quruntul, stands 13 km/8 miles north-west of el-Maghtas.

'As soon as Jesus was baptized, he went up out of the water. At that moment heaven was opened, and he saw the Spirit of God descending like a dove and lighting on him. And a voice from heaven said, "This is my Son, whom I love; with him I am well pleased."'
Matthew 3:16–17

WADI QELT
ST GEORGE'S MONASTERY

The steep cliffs of the Wadi Qelt
provide a dramatic setting for the
Greek Orthodox monastery of
St George of Koziba. During the
fourth to sixth centuries AD well
over 100 monasteries sprang up in
the desert east of Jerusalem. Only
a few exist today. St George's is an
excellent example and welcomes
visitors.

The Wadi Qelt was probably the
route taken by Joshua's men when
they were sent into the hills from
Jericho to spy out Ai (Joshua 7:2).
The stream which flows through the
wadi was an important source of
water for New Testament Jericho,
the excavated remains of which lie
on both sides of the wadi where it
opens into the Jordan valley. The site
today is called Tulul Abu el-Alaiq.

The present Monastery of St George was built 1878–1901, but there was a monastery here in the fifth to seventh centuries and again in the twelfth to fourteenth centuries.

QUMRAN

The ruins of Khirbet Qumran, 1km/0.6 miles from the north-west shore of the Dead Sea, were excavated in 1951 after several ancient scrolls had been found in nearby caves. These scrolls were part of that collection now known as the Dead Sea Scrolls. The ruins turned out to be a complex of buildings used by the community which produced the scrolls. The community was a branch of the Jewish sect known as the Essenes, and they lived in this area from about 140BC to AD68, when their settlement was destroyed by the Romans. At its peak the desert community had over 300 members. While some of the Dead Sea Scrolls are copies of Old Testament books, others contain the distinctive beliefs of the Qumran sect. From these we learn that they lived a monastic style of life, believing themselves to be the true Israel, destined to play a leading role at the approaching end of the age. The excavated ruins of their community compound, with its kitchens, refectory, council chamber, workshops, reservoirs and ritual baths, testify to their organization and disciplined piety.

The excavated remains of the buildings at Qumran are shown here, looking south. One of the caves which contained the Dead Sea Scrolls is situated at the end of the eroded spur to the right.

EN GEDI

In places the arid western shore of the Dead Sea is transformed into patches of green by freshwater springs. The most beautiful of these is En Gedi. Water from a hot spring cascades down the cliffs to feed a semi-tropical oasis. Vegetation runs riot, and in biblical times vineyards flourished there.

When David was being hunted down by Saul, he hid in a cave at En Gedi. He had an opportunity to kill Saul but refrained, and when he revealed himself, there was an emotional confrontation between the two men.

'After Saul returned from pursuing the Philistines, he was told, "David is in the Desert of En Gedi". So Saul took 3,000 chosen men from all Israel and set out to look for David and his men near the Crags of the Wild Goats.'
1 Samuel 24:1–2

The picture shows the waterfall in the Nahal David at En Gedi. The area around the oasis is now a nature reserve where many wild animals and birds can be seen—including ibexes, the 'wild goats' of 1 Samuel 24:2.

MASADA

Separated by a deep ravine from the cliffs on the western shore of the Dead Sea, the spectacular crag of Masada is an almost impregnable natural fortress. It rises some 360m/1,200ft above the desert plain and its top is a plateau shaped like the deck of a ship, 540m/1,800ft long and 225m/750ft across at its widest point. There is no certain reference to Masada in the Bible, but it may be 'the stronghold' mentioned in 1 Samuel chapter 22, where David and his men lived in hiding. In the first century BC Herod the Great equipped it on a grand scale with fortifications and palaces. In AD66, at the beginning of the Jewish revolt against Rome, it was captured from Roman forces by Jewish rebels known as the Sicarii (not, as often stated, the Zealots). Masada was the last rebel stronghold to be taken by the Romans after the destruction of Jerusalem in AD70. It fell in the spring of AD74 after a siege of some months. All but a handful of its 967 occupants (men, women and children) ended their lives in a suicide pact when the fortress's capture became inevitable. Visitors to this atmospheric place can see the partially restored remains of the buildings erected by Herod and later used by the rebels, as well as traces of a Byzantine monastic settlement of the fourth to fifth centuries AD.

The lofty rock of Masada seen here from the east was the scene of the tragic final act in the Jewish revolt against Rome, AD66–74.

The northern half of the plateau of Masada is viewed here from the west. On the left of the picture the remains of Herod's northern palace and storerooms can be seen. Rising up from the centre foreground is the core of the huge ramp built by the Romans to assault the walls on the western side. On the plateau just to the right are the remains of Herod's western palace.

BETHLEHEM

The name Bethlehem means
'House of Bread', reflecting its
location in a fertile grain-growing
area west of the Judean wilderness.
It was always a small place and even
as 'the city of David' it had no
special status. However, as the
birthplace of Jesus it became a
focus of Christian devotion and
pilgrimage. From the early second
century AD, tradition identified a
cave there as the exact spot where
Jesus was born, and in AD330 the
emperor Constantine founded the
Church of the Nativity over it. The
great Christian scholar Jerome
settled in Bethlehem later that
century, and an important monastic
community grew up around him.
A tradition of uncertain value
identifies one of the caves in the
complex beneath the Church as his
study.

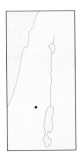

When the people of Judah longed for another king of David's stature, the prophet Micah predicted that the Messiah would be born in Bethlehem. This was fulfilled when the birth of Jesus took place there. It has become traditional to think that Jesus was born in a stable because Mary and Joseph were turned away from the local inn. However, Luke 2:7 more correctly means that Mary 'laid him in a manger because there was no space for them in the room'. Peasant houses usually contained an area where the animals were sheltered at night, and Luke is probably saying that Mary and Joseph withdrew there because the only other room in the small house was too crowded for the birth to take place in privacy. This does not contradict the tradition that Jesus' birthplace was a cave; even today some peasant houses are built against caves which serve as their rear quarters. We should not forget that the great miracle of the incarnation occurred in very ordinary circumstances.

'But you, Bethlehem Ephrathah, though you are small among the clans of Judah, out of you will come for me one who will be ruler over Israel, whose origins are from of old, from ancient times.'
Micah 5:2

The spaciousness of the Church of the Nativity is belied by its unimpressive entrance. In the sixth century AD the emperor Justinian replaced Constantine's building with a much larger one, and the present Church is largely Justinian's work, restored and modified several times over the intervening centuries. Fragments of the mosaic floor of Constantine's Church still survive beneath the present one and are displayed to visitors.

SOLOMON'S POOLS

About 12km/7.5 miles south-west of Jerusalem, next to the site of Old Testament Etam, three reservoirs lie in a wooded valley. They take their name from a tradition which links this spot with Solomon's pleasure-gardens. Whether the place had pools as long ago as Solomon's day is unknown, but certainly by Herod's reign, and perhaps much earlier, water channelled from springs to the south was stored here to supplement the water-supply of Jerusalem. A long, winding aqueduct carried the water to cisterns within the Temple Mount.

The tradition linking Solomon with this place is ancient. Writing in the first century, the Jewish historian Josephus said that Solomon paid regular visits to some well-watered gardens at Etam. Later, the spring at nearby Artas was identified with that referred to in the Song of Solomon chapter 4.

These reservoirs were an important part of Jerusalem's water-supply right up to the twentieth century. Their present form is modern, but there have been reservoirs here for at least 2,000 years.

'I made gardens and parks and planted all kinds of fruit trees in them. I made reservoirs to water groves of flourishing trees.' Ecclesiastes 2:5–6

H E R O D I U M

Herod the Great strengthened his kingdom with several fortresses, all of them sumptuously equipped. Herodium, 12km/7.5 miles south of Jerusalem, was a magnificent fortified palace set in the top of a hill. The upper part of the hill is entirely artificial and the whole concept is evidence of Herod's bold imagination. At the foot of the hill was another palace complex with a pool and gardens. This was the focus of a settlement called Herodia.

Herodium is not mentioned in the Bible, but it may have been the place from which Herod's troops were despatched to kill the male offspring of Bethlehem, only 6km/3.75 miles away. Herod died at Jericho in 4BC, not long after this event, and he was carried to Herodium for burial. His tomb has never been found.

The aerial view of Herodium from the north-west shows the remains of Herod's fortified palace nestling in its artificial hilltop.

This view across the excavated remains of the hilltop citadel (inset above right) looks towards Bethlehem, which can just be seen on the skyline.

HEBRON

Situated in the heart of the Judean highlands, biblical Hebron lay on a hill overlooking the present town. In 20BC Herod the Great built a magnificent wall to surround the traditional Cave of Machpelah, and this is still perfectly preserved, though marred by a crenellated top and other late additions. Because of its links with Abraham the site is sacred to Muslims as well as to Jews and Christians, and the town shifted to this location during the Arab period.

Abraham stayed often by the Oaks of Mamre near Hebron, and it was probably there that God made a covenant with him. He bought the nearby Cave of Machpelah from the people of Hebron for use as a family tomb. Centuries later, when David became king of Judah, he ruled from Hebron for seven-and-a-half years before turning Jerusalem into the new capital of all Israel.

Herod's enclosure was made into a mosque in the Arab period, and is known to Muslims as the Haram el-Khalil ('Enclosure of the Friend'), because of Abraham's status as 'the friend of God'. Isaiah 41:8

'Then Abraham breathed his last and died at a good old age. . . His sons Isaac and Ishmael buried him in the Cave of Machpelah near Mamre, in the field. . . Abraham had bought from the Hittites. There Abraham was buried with his wife Sarah.' Genesis 25:8–10

BEERSHEBA

Beersheba is situated in the dry region known as the Negev, and in biblical times it marked the southern limit of Israel's settled territory; hence the length of the land is summed up in Judges chapter 20 by the phrase 'from Dan to Beersheba'. The settlement of Abraham's day probably lies beneath the modern town of Beer Sheva. About 3km/2 miles to the west stands Tell es-Saba (or Tel Sheba), the ruin-mound of a city which flourished during the eleventh to eighth centuries BC.

The excavated mound of the city founded at Beersheba in the eleventh century BC is shown above. A well by the mound dates from about the same time and is therefore too recent to be Abraham's. If Abraham's well still exists, it could be one of several ancient wells in the vicinity of the modern town.

_____

_____

_____

_____

_____

_____

_____

_____

_____

_____

Abraham, Isaac and Jacob all had connections with Beersheba. The place acquired its name (Well of Seven or Well of the Oath) when a dispute arose over the well which Abraham had dug there. Isaac later re-dug and renamed the same well, and his family was settled at Beersheba when Jacob tricked Esau out of his blessing. Many years later, as an old man on his way south to Egypt, Jacob had a vision of God at Beersheba, recorded in Genesis chapter 46.

'Then Abraham complained to Abimelech about a well of water that Abimelech's servants had seized. . . So Abraham brought sheep and cattle and gave them to Abimelech, and the two men made a treaty. Abraham set apart seven ewe lambs from the flock. . . So that place was called Beersheba, because the two men swore an oath there.'
Genesis 21:25, 27–28, 31

51

JACOB'S WELL

Jacob's Well stands at the eastern end of modern Nablus and little over 0.5km/0.3 miles from the site of Old Testament Shechem. To the south-west rises Mount Gerizim, where the Samaritan temple was built in the fourth century BC. The temple was destroyed in 128BC by the Jewish king John Hyrcanus, intensifying the hatred between Samaritans and Jews.

When Jesus spoke to the Samaritan woman at Jacob's Well he broke with convention; Samaritans and Jews were separated by bitter prejudice. On recognizing Jesus as a prophet, she asked him to settle the dispute which most deeply divided them: should God be worshipped in Jerusalem or on Mount Gerizim? When Jesus spoke of himself as the Messiah the woman believed, and so did other Samaritans whom she brought to meet him.

'Jesus answered, "Everyone who drinks this water will be thirsty again, but whoever drinks the water I give him will never thirst. Indeed, the water I give him will become in him a spring of water welling up to eternal life."'
John 4:13–14

By the first century AD this well was already associated with Jacob, who bought land at Shechem. Since the fourth century there has been a succession of churches on the site, commemorating Jesus' meeting with the Samaritan woman. The present church, begun in 1914, remains incomplete. The well, located in the crypt, is 35m/114ft deep.

SAMARIA – SEBASTE

Separated from the surrounding hills by broad, fertile valleys, the hill of Samaria affords commanding views in all directions. On a clear day even the coast is visible. Around 876BC the hill was chosen by Omri as the location for Israel's new capital, and it retained that status for 150 years. In subsequent centuries Samaria was the seat of Assyrian and Persian governors and then suffered two major destructions. In 30BC the emperor Octavian granted the town to Herod the Great, who restored it to splendour and greatness. Herod rebuilt it with all the features of a Roman city—theatre, forum, stadium, colonnaded street and fine temples. He renamed it Sebaste (Greek for Augusta) in honour of Octavian, who took the name Augustus in 27BC. Its Greek name is still preserved in the name of the Arab village of Sebastiye. On the crown of the hill Israelite, Hellenistic and Roman remains mingle in bewildering profusion.

These remains are of the wall of the Israelite royal palace, built by Omri and Ahab on Samaria's summit, with a glimpse of the distant hills beyond.

The steps of a Roman temple built above Israelite remains on the acropolis. Originally built by Herod the Great to Augustus, it was restored by the emperor Septimius Severus around AD200 and the steps belong to that later period.

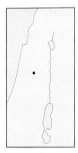

As the capital of the northern kingdom, Samaria was denounced by the prophets Amos and Hosea for its leading role in Israel's idolatry. In fulfilment of their dire warnings the city was destroyed by the Assyrians in 722BC, and the northern kingdom came to an end. In the fifth century BC the governor of Samaria under the Persians, Sanballat the Horonite, opposed Nehemiah's attempts to strengthen Jerusalem. A descendant and namesake of Sanballat later founded the temple of the Samaritans on Mount Gerizim. His link with Samaria may explain the name of this sect, which was otherwise associated with the area around Shechem (see page 52).

'Omri became king of Israel, and he reigned for twelve years. . . He bought the hill of Samaria from Shemer for two talents of silver and built a city on the hill, calling it Samaria. . .'
1 Kings 16:23–24

Beth Shan lies in the well-watered valley of the River Harod, 5km/ 3 miles west of where it enters the Jordan. The Harod valley joins the eastern end of the valley of Jezreel, which means that Beth Shan controlled the major east-west route across the country. A town grew up here around 3000BC and it remained important for over 4,000 years.

There is little to be seen on the ruin-mound of the Old Testament city, and the site's most impressive monument is a very well-preserved Roman theatre from about AD200.

When the Israelites entered Canaan they could not conquer Beth Shan, whose chariot forces dominated the plains. From the fifteenth century BC the city was controlled by Egypt, but when Egypt's power declined it was briefly held by the Philistines; they displayed the bodies of Saul and Jonathan there after defeating Israel on Mount Gilboa. But the city was in Israelite hands by Solomon's reign, probably as a result of David's conquests. In New Testament times (when it was called Scythopolis) it was the largest city in the league known as the Decapolis.

'When the Philistines came to strip the dead, they found Saul and his three sons fallen on Mount Gilboa. . . They put his armour in the temple of the Ashtoreths and fastened his body to the wall of Beth Shan.' 1 Samuel 31:8 and 10

CAESAREA

The port of Caesarea, 37km/23 miles south of Mount Carmel, was one of Herod the Great's triumphs Between 22 and 9BC he turned a minor coastal station into a major Mediterranean port. In recent years underwater archaeology has brought to light the brilliant engineering feats by which its fine 3.5-acre harbour was created. Herod's Caesarea became the provincial capital of Judea and the official residence of the Roman procurators who governed it. Pontius Pilate lived there during his procuratorship (AD26–36), residing in Jerusalem only during the festivals. During a brief respite from Roman governors, Caesarea was the home of the Jewish king Herod Agrippa I. The incident in Acts chapter 12, which resulted in his death, took place (according to the historian Josephus) in the theatre, which has been recently restored. Caesarea continued to be an important city for centuries, and has impressive remains from the Byzantine and Crusader periods.

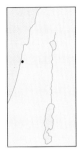

Ancient columns, washed by the sea, lie near the remains of the harbour's southern breakwater.

Caesarea holds a special place in the history of Gentile Christianity. The Roman centurion Cornelius was converted there, and Paul visited the city during the missionary journeys recorded in Acts chapters 18 and 21. He was tried there by the procurator Felix and imprisoned for two years (possibly AD59–61). Eventually, after defending himself before Festus (Felix's successor) and Agrippa II, Paul was sent by ship from Caesarea to be tried in Rome by the emperor.

'While Peter was still speaking. . . the Holy Spirit came on all who heard the message. The circumcised believers who had come with Peter were astonished that the gift of the Holy Spirit had been poured out even on the Gentiles.'
Acts 10:44–5

MOUNT CARMEL

The majestic Carmel range extends some 25km/16 miles north-west from the hills of Samaria to the coast, where it becomes a promontory creating the Bay of Haifa. At its highest point (Rom Hacarmel) the ridge reaches 548m/1,798ft. The Egyptians, Phoenicians and Romans all regarded Carmel as a sacred mountain. A small monastery now stands on the traditional site of Elijah's contest with the prophets of Baal.

In biblical times the Carmel range had many more trees than today, and the Old Testament sometimes mentions its wooded heights alongside those of Lebanon.
Isaiah 33:9; 35:2

The impressive ridge came to symbolize strength, abundance and beauty in the Old Testament. Historically it is best known as the scene of the crucial contest between Elijah and the 450 prophets of Baal. The exact site of this dramatic conflict is traditionally located at Muhraqa, a peak of 482m/1,581ft. The sea can be seen from this spot and it overlooks the Jezreel Valley where the brook Kishon flows. It was by this brook that Elijah killed the prophets of Baal after their false worship had been discredited.

'Then the fire of the Lord fell and burned up the sacrifice. . . When all the people saw this, they fell prostrate and cried, "The Lord, he is God!"'
1 Kings 18:38–9

JEZREEL VALLEY

North-east of the Carmel range the broad valley of Jezreel (or Esdraelon) sweeps inland from the Bay of Haifa. Between the hills of Lower Galilee and the Gilboa mountains it connects with the Harod valley west of Beth Shan, forming an important east-west route between the Jordan and the coastal plain. It also contains productive farming land, and in biblical times had some important cities along its fringes.

A patchwork of fields is evidence of the fertility which gave the town and valley their ancient name; Jezreel means 'God sows'.

_____

_____

_____

_____

_____

_____

_____

At the eastern end of the valley lay the Old Testament town of Jezreel, where King Ahab had a royal residence (though his capital was Samaria). When Ahab wanted to buy Naboth's vineyard and Naboth refused to part with it, Queen Jezebel had Naboth executed on a trumped-up charge and confiscated his vineyard for the royal estates. Later, however, Jezebel herself came to a gruesome end at Jezreel.

'Then the word of the Lord came to Elijah the Tishbite: "Go down to meet Ahab king of Israel, who rules in Samaria. He is now in Naboth's vineyard, where he has gone to take possession of it. Say to him, 'This is what the Lord says: Have you not murdered a man and seized his property?' . . . And also concerning Jezebel the Lord says: 'Dogs will devour Jezebel by the wall of Jezreel'.'"
1 Kings 21:17–19, 23

MEGIDDO

The city of Megiddo overlooked one of history's great battlefields—the northern end of a vital pass through the Carmel range. Its strategic position ensured its importance for nearly 3,000 years (roughly 3300–500BC). Among the many visible remains are those of a gateway from Solomon's time (similar to ones at Hazor and Gezer) and some buildings once thought to be Solomon's stables but now dated to the time of Ahab (ninth century BC). Also of Ahab's time is an impressive tunnel leading to the city's spring.

Looking across the foundations of one half of Solomon's six-chambered gate at Megiddo, with the valley of Jezreel beyond.

The Israelites initially failed to wrest Megiddo from the Canaanites and the Bible does not tell us when it finally came into their hands. It probably fell to David. Solomon rebuilt it as an administrative centre. About 350 years later, Josiah was killed there while trying to hold the pass against an Egyptian army on its way north. As befits a historic battlefield, it features in the book of Revelation as Armageddon (Mount of Megiddo), the scene of the last battle of all.

'. . . They go out to the kings of the whole world, to gather them for the battle on the great day of God Almighty. . . Then they gathered the kings together to the place that in Hebrew is called Armageddon.' Revelation 16:14 and 16

MOUNT TABOR

Standing 8km/5 miles east of Nazareth, the smooth dome of Mount Tabor rises to 411m/1,348ft above the surrounding plain. Its summit offers magnificent views. Because of its commanding position and strategic importance (close to the valley of Jezreel) the summit has frequently been fortified. The remains of a fortification wall built by the Jews in AD67, during their war with Rome, can still be seen.

With its steep slopes and smooth outline, this isolated limestone mountain is an imposing sight from any direction.

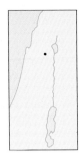

In Old Testament times the tribal boundaries of Issachar, Zebulun and Naphtali met at Mount Tabor. It was where Barak gathered the men of Zebulun and Naphtali to fight against the troops of Sisera; when Sisera's 900 chariots became bogged down in the plain at the foot of the mountain, his army was quickly routed by Barak's forces. Since the fourth century AD Mount Tabor has been identified as the mountain where Jesus was transfigured, and a modern basilica near the summit commemorates that event.

'Barak went down Mount Tabor, followed by 10,000. At Barak's advance, the Lord routed Sisera and all his chariots and army by the sword, and Sisera abandoned his chariot and fled on foot.' Judges 4:14–15

NAZARETH

The modern town of Nazareth nestles in a high valley among the hills of Lower Galilee. Its biblical counterpart probably lay higher up the hill to the west. Relatively secluded, it was a totally insignificant village until its associations with Mary, Joseph and Jesus made it the goal of Christian pilgrims. It does not appear in the Old Testament, and there is no mention of it outside the Bible until the second century AD.

In Luke's Gospel, Nazareth is the home of both Mary and Joseph before the birth of Jesus, and all four Gospels agree that it was the place where Jesus grew up and lived until the beginning of his ministry. He is frequently referred to as 'Jesus of Nazareth'. However, its people violently rejected him, and he subsequently moved to Capernaum.

'He went into the synagogue, as was his custom, and he stood up to read. . . He found the place where it is written: "The Spirit of the Lord is on me, because he has anointed me to preach good news to the poor. He has sent me to proclaim freedom for the prisoners and recovery of sight for the blind, to release the oppressed, to proclaim the year of the Lord's favour." . . . and he began by saying to them, "Today this scripture is fulfilled in your hearing".'
Luke 4:16–21

When Jesus lived at Nazareth it was a
sleepy backwater. Its isolation and lack
of importance explain Nathanael's
exclamation in John chapter 1: 'Nazareth!
Can anything good come from there?'

SEA OF GALILEE

This large, attractive lake has many names: the Sea of Chinnereth in the Old Testament, the Sea of Galilee, Sea of Tiberius and Lake Gennesaret in the New Testament. The warm climate resulting from its low altitude (about 210m/689ft below sea-level), combined with a fertile soil, made the surrounding hills a prosperous agricultural region in New Testament times. After the fall of Jerusalem in AD70, Galilee became the focus of Jewish settlement in Palestine and several important synagogues were built in the lakeside towns.

The Sea of Galilee is fed by the Jordan and several springs, and is about 20km/12 miles long and 13km/8 miles wide. Catching and exporting fish remains an important industry, and fishing is still made hazardous by the strong winds which rush down suddenly from the surrounding hills.

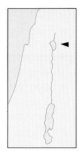

The books of 1 and 2 Kings record that in Old Testament times the whole region of Galilee suffered disastrous foreign invasions. However, Isaiah predicted a reversal of its fortunes: 'in the future God will honour Galilee of the Gentiles.' It was therefore fitting that most of Jesus' life was lived in this area. His Galilean ministry was in fact concentrated around the lake. His first disciples were fishermen and he taught by its shores. The lake itself was the scene of three miracles which pointed to Jesus' divinity: the miraculous catch of fish, stilling the storm and walking on the water.

'He got up and rebuked the wind and the raging waters; the storm subsided and all was calm. . . In fear and amazement they asked one another, "Who is this? He commands even the winds and the water, and they obey him."' Luke 8:24–5

CAPERNAUM

The fishing village of Capernaum lay on the north shore of the Sea of Galilee, not far from where the Jordan enters it. In Jesus' day it was a border town (the Jordan being the border between Galilee and the territory of Philip the Tetrarch) with a customs post. Levi (Matthew) collected the revenues there before Jesus called him. It also had a small Roman garrison, whose centurion had built the town's synagogue. Parts of the Capernaum Jesus knew have now been exposed by excavations.

The partially restored synagogue at Capernaum dates from the fourth century AD, but it was constructed on the same spot as the synagogue of Jesus' day.

Jesus made Capernaum the base for his Galilean ministry. He called his first disciples at the lakeside and taught in its synagogue. Not far from the site of the synagogue are the remains of the traditional house of Peter, where Jesus stayed and to which crowds flocked to hear him and to be healed. (This house seems to have been used as a church as early as the first century AD, and so stands a good chance of being authentic.)

'That evening after sunset the people brought to Jesus all the sick and demon-possessed. The whole town gathered at the door, and Jesus healed many who had various diseases.' Mark 1:32–4

TABGHA (HEPTAPEGON)

Many incidents in Jesus' Galilean ministry are not precisely located by the Gospel accounts. For some of these, later Christian tradition has supplied sites which may or may not be correct. In the fourth–fifth centuries three churches stood at Tabgha, commemorating the Feeding of the Five Thousand, the Sermon on the Mount, and Jesus' post-resurrection appearance recorded in John 21. The modern Church of the Multiplication of the Loaves and Fishes is a reconstruction of the church of the Byzantine period, dedicated in 1982. It incorporates the remains of the original, including some outstanding mosaics.

This Byzantine mosaic of the loaves and fishes is now relocated in front of the high altar of the restored church.

It is evident from the Gospel accounts that the Feeding of the Five Thousand occurred at an isolated, grassy place near the shore of the Sea of Galilee. Tabgha (from the Greek 'heptapegon', meaning 'seven springs') 4km/2.5 miles west of Capernaum, certainly fits these requirements. However, the reference to Bethsaida in Luke chapter 9 favours a location east of the Jordan. More important than the location of the miracle is its significance. In John's account it points to Jesus himself as 'the bread of life'.

'Taking the five loaves and the two fish and looking up to heaven, he gave thanks. . . They all ate and were satisfied, and the disciples picked up twelve basketfuls of broken pieces that were left over. The number of those who ate was about 5,000 men, besides women and children.'
Matthew 14:19–21

MOUNT OF THE BEATITUDES

On the opposite side of the road from the church which commemorates the Feeding of the Five Thousand (see Tabgha) stand some ancient ruins. These are the remains of a small monastery and a church of the fourth–seventh centuries AD. Beneath the church is a cave where, according to a tradition current in the fourth century, Jesus spoke the Beatitudes. This church has now been replaced by a modern one built further up the hill, and it is the site of this church which is today known as the Mount of the Beatitudes. The church is octagonal, its sides corresponding to the eight Beatitudes of Matthew chapter 5 and it provides a superb view over the Sea of Galilee.

This is the view from the Mount of the Beatitudes, looking towards the Sea of Galilee. Several places associated with Jesus' Galilean ministry can be seen from here.

The Sermon on the Mount (Matthew 5–7) was teaching intended for Jesus' close followers. When Jesus went up into the hills he was therefore withdrawing from the huge crowds which were following him, taking his disciples aside for a time of more intimate instruction. The Sermon contains some of the most radical and challenging aspects of Jesus' teaching, and the Beatitudes sum up the qualities which together should make up the Christian's character.

'Large crowds from Galilee, the Decapolis, Jerusalem, Judea and the region across the Jordan followed him. Now when he saw the crowds, he went up on a mountainside and sat down. His disciples came to him, and he began to teach them. . .' Matthew 4:25–5:2

HAZOR

Situated 15km/9 miles north of the Sea of Galilee, the impressive ruin-mound of Hazor conceals a history stretching back to about 2700BC. Hazor lay where an important pass through the mountains of Galilee formed a crossroads with the main route from Egypt to northern Mesopotamia. From about 1700–1230BC it was the largest city in Canaan. It covered over 200 acres and had a population of 30–40,000. Rebuilt on a much smaller scale, Hazor thrived again in the time of the Israelite monarchy. The remains of a gateway from Solomon's time can still be seen, and also a storehouse and water-shaft from about a century later.

Looking east from the mound of Hazor, the excavated remains of a pillared storehouse from the time of Ahab (ninth century BC) can be seen in the foreground.

In the time of Joshua, Hazor was the vast Canaanite city described above, and headed all the city-states of northern Canaan. In spite of its strength, Joshua captured and destroyed it. However, by the time of Deborah it had revived as a Canaanite centre and had to be defeated a second time. Solomon rebuilt it as an Israelite city; it was destroyed by the Assyrians in 734BC and never regained its importance.

'All these kings joined forces and made camp together. . . So Joshua and his whole army came against them suddenly at the Waters of Merom and attacked them, and the Lord gave them into the hand of Israel. . . At that time Joshua turned back and captured Hazor and put its king to the sword. (Hazor had been the head of all these kingdoms.)'
Joshua 11:5, 7–8, 10

CAESAREA PHILIPPI (BANYAS)

This beautiful district at the foot of Mount Hermon is noted for its abundant spring, which is the chief source of the Jordan. Under the Greeks the town here was called Paneas, because the cave at the outlet of the spring was a shrine to the nature-god Pan. (The modern name Banyas is a corruption of this.) The town was developed by Herod the Great, and later by Philip the Tetrarch, who renamed it Caesarea after the emperor Augustus Caesar. It was known as Caesarea Philippi (Caesarea of Philip) to distinguish it from Caesarea on the coast. There are important Crusader remains there, as well as scattered blocks and columns from the city of New Testament times.

The region of Caesarea Philippi was the scene of a great turning-point in the ministry of Jesus. He asked his disciples what people were saying of him, and after hearing their replies he pressed them for their own opinion. It was then that Peter made his inspired confession: 'You are the Christ, the Son of the living God.' After that, Jesus began to teach his disciples that he would have to suffer and die in order to fulfil God's purpose.

'From that time on Jesus began to explain to his disciples that he must go to Jerusalem and suffer many things at the hands of the elders, chief priests and teachers of the law, and that he must be killed and on the third day be raised to life.' Matthew 16:21

Streams flowing from the copious spring at Banyas provided a delightful setting for a Roman city, capital of the territory of Philip the Tetrarch. It was probably the northernmost limit of Jesus' ministry.

MOUNT HERMON

Mount Hermon is the southernmost of the Anti-Lebanon mountains. It is not a single mountain but a range of peaks ('the heights of Hermon' of Psalm 42), the highest of which rises to 3,030m/9,232ft. The peaks are snow-covered most of the time, with some snow remaining even through summer.

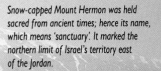

Snow-capped Mount Hermon was held sacred from ancient times; hence its name, which means 'sanctuary'. It marked the northern limit of Israel's territory east of the Jordan.

Although Mount Hermon is not named in the New Testament, many scholars think that one of its peaks was the 'high mountain' where Jesus was transfigured. Tradition locates this event on Mount Tabor but this lies 70km/44 miles from Caesarea Philippi, whereas the Gospels mention no long journey from that place to the mount of transfiguration. Caesarea Philippi lies at the south-western end of Mount Hermon.

'After six days Jesus took Peter, James and John with him and led them up a high mountain, where they were all alone. There he was transfigured before them. His clothes became dazzling white, whiter than anyone in the world could bleach them. . . Then a cloud appeared and enveloped them, and a voice came from the cloud: "This is my Son, whom I love. Listen to him!"'
Mark 9:2–3, 7

85

CLOTHING

While light clothing is usually adequate during the spring and summer months, there can be surprising temperature differences. The hills are generally cooler than the Jordan valley, especially early in the morning and in the evening, when a warm pullover may be needed as a protection against chilly breezes. Temperatures are highest around the Sea of Galilee, along the Jordan valley and by the Dead Sea. In the basin of the Sea of Galilee the humidity can make summer nights uncomfortably hot in the absence of air conditioning. In view of the variety of conditions, it is best to carry layers of clothing which can be added or removed as necessary. In the winter months there is still a good deal of sunshine, but also a great deal of rain, and in the Jerusalem hills there are occasional heavy falls of snow. Warm clothing, waterproofs and suitable footwear are therefore essential for visits during this period.

Maximum and minimum temperatures are as follows:

	spring (March)	summer (July)	winter (November)
Jerusalem	52–64 F	66–82 F	54–66 F
	11–18 C	19–28 C	12–19 C
Tiberias	57–79 F	77–99 F	63–81 F
	14–26 C	25–37 C	17–27 C
Eilat	66–82 F	84–104 F	57–82 F
	19–28 C	29–40 C	15–28 C

When visiting mosques, synagogues, churches and monasteries, it is essential to dress correctly. Failure to do so will mean exclusion from the site. Women must have their shoulders covered, and must wear skirts that cover the knee (not trousers). Women may have to cover their heads as well. Men should wear long trousers, and when visiting synagogues they will usually be provided with cardboard skull-caps.

Sturdy rubber soles are advisable for all excursions out of the modern towns. Away from the beaten track, long trousers are sometimes necessary to protect the legs against prickly vegetation. A canteen of water should always be taken on trips to the hotter places (Jericho, the Dead Sea and Masada, for example), and no visitor should venture into desert areas without an experienced guide.

OPENING TIMES OF MUSEUMS AND ARCHAEOLOGICAL SITES

Several important archaeological sites are now National Parks, and visitors planning to see a number of these will make a significant saving if they purchase a general admission ticket. Some National Parks sell these at their ticket office; or they can be obtained from the National Parks Authority, 3 Het Street, Hakiriya, Tel Aviv.

Museums in Jerusalem

Israel Museum Ruppin Street (Rehov Ruppin), opposite the Knesset (parliament) building. Its various sections trace Jewish life, history and art through the centuries. Many items of biblical interest are to be seen in the Bronfman Archaeological Museum, and the Shrine of the Book contains some of the Dead Sea Scrolls.
10 am–5 pm Sunday, Monday, Wednesday and Thursday; 4 pm–10 pm Tuesday; 10 am–2 pm Friday and Saturday.

Dor Va-Dor Museum 58 King George V Street (Rehov Hamelech George), within Heichal Shlomo. Specializes in Jewish religious art and artefacts.
9 am–1 pm Sunday–Thursday; 9 am–noon Friday.

Agricultural Museum 13 Rehov Heleni Hamalka, off Rehov Yafo. Displays farming implements from 2,000 years ago to the present.
7.30 am–3 pm Sunday–Thursday; 7.30 am–2 pm Friday.

Islamic Museum Entrance just south of the Moors' Gate, Western Wall. Exhibits relating to the history of the Haram esh-Sharif.
9 am–4 pm Saturday–Thursday.

Rockefeller Museum Nur-ed-Din, north of the north-east corner of the Old City. Archaeological exhibits covering the period from the Stone Age to the eighteenth century.
10 am–6 pm Sunday–Thursday; 10 am–2 pm Friday and Saturday.

Model of Herodian Jerusalem In grounds of the Holyland Hotel, Uziel Street. A spectacular 1:50 scale model of Jerusalem in the first century. Although some of the interpretations embodied in the model are debatable, it is to be highly recommended as an aid to visualizing the city as it was in New Testament times.
9 am–5 pm Saturday–Thursday (but admission tickets for Saturday have to be bought during the week); 9 am–4 pm Friday.

Tel Aviv/Jaffa (Yafo)

Ha'aretz Museum Complex Derech Haifa. Archaeological exhibits, ancient coins and glassware.
9 am–4 pm Sunday–Thursday; 9 am–1 pm Friday; 10 am–2 pm Saturday.

Museum of Antiquities 10 Mifratz Shlomo Street. Archaeological exhibits, especially from sites in the neighbourhood.
9 am–4 pm Sunday–Thursday; 9 am–1 pm Friday; 10 am–2 pm Saturday.

Bet Ha-Tanakh (Bible House) 16 Sderot Rothschild. A collection of books, manuscripts and paintings relating to the Hebrew scriptures.

Haifa

The Haifa Museum 26 Shabbetay Levi Street. Notable for its collection of ancient art up to the seventh century.
10 am–1 pm Sunday–Thursday and Saturday; also 6 pm–9 pm Tuesday, Thursday and Saturday.

Haifa is well-endowed with museums catering for specialist tastes; there is a Maritime Museum, a Prehistory Museum, an Edible Oil Museum and the Dagon Museum devoted to the history of man's cultivation of grain-crops.

Beer Sheva

Negev Museum Derech Ha'atzmaut. Exhibits show the history of settlement in the Negev.
8 am–2 pm Sunday–Thursday; also 4.30 pm–7 pm on Wednesday; 8 am–1 pm Friday; 10 am–1 pm Saturday.

OPENING TIMES OF SITES MENTIONED IN THE *TRAVEL DIARY OF THE HOLY LAND*

NB These may be subject to occasional changes.

Monastery of St George, Wadi Qelt: 8 am–5 pm

Qumran: 8 am–5 pm (closes 4 pm Friday)

Masada: 6.30 am–3.30 pm

Herodium: 8 am–5 pm. (This applies only to the excavations at the top of the hill; the remains at the base of the hill are accessible at all times.)

Jacob's Well: 8 am–noon; 2–4 pm

Samaria-Sebaste: 8 am–5 pm

Beth Shan: 8 am–4 pm (closes 3 pm Friday)

Caesarea: 8 am–4 pm (closes 3 pm Friday)

Megiddo (including the National Park Museum adjacent to the mound); 8 am–5 pm (closes 4 pm Friday)

Capernaum: 8.30 am–4.15 pm

Tabgha: the Church of the Multiplication of the Loaves and Fishes is open 7 am–5 pm; the Church of the Primacy of Peter is open 8.30 am–4 pm

Hazor: the Hazor Museum, across the road from the mound, displays finds from the excavations; open 8 am–4 pm.

PEOPLES AND FAITHS

The complex history of the Holy Land is reflected today in the variety of its peoples and faiths.

JEWS AND ARABS, ISRAELIS AND PALESTINIANS

If we define the Holy Land as the combined area of the state of Israel and the occupied territories (the West Bank and the Gaza Strip), its total population is over 5.5 million. Of this figure, about 3.5 million are Jews. The majority of these belong to families which have settled in the Holy Land during the last 100 years, though the Jews trace their claim to the land back to biblical times. Even the great many modern Jews who have a purely secular outlook still feel a powerful attachment to the land. The Holy Land's other 2 million inhabitants are Palestinian Arabs; it has been their homeland for centuries. Within the state of Israel the population of about 3,900,000 is approximately 84% Jewish and 16% Arab. All these inhabitants of the state of Israel, Jews and Arabs, are Israeli citizens. In the occupied territories the total population of about 1,600,000 is 97% Arab and 3% Jewish.

The term 'Palestinian', as used today, refers to all those Arabs for whom the Holy Land is their ancestral home. Many of them no longer live there, however, but are refugees settled in over a dozen countries, chiefly in Jordan, Lebanon, Kuwait and Syria. For Palestinians their homeland is still 'Palestine'. Technically, however, there has been no such political entity as 'Palestine' since 1948, and the term is therefore a politically sensitive one. Visitors should make every effort to avoid giving offence by the way they refer to the land and its peoples.

THE FAITHS OF THE HOLY LAND

The world's great monotheistic religions, Judaism, Christianity and Islam, are all represented in the Holy Land. Jerusalem is sacred to all three: for Jews it is the place chosen by God to be the site of the temple, his special dwelling-place; for Christians it is the place where Jesus died and rose again; for Muslims it is their third holiest site, significant as the place where

Abraham offered his son and from where Muhammad made his night journey to heaven.

Although visitors from the West tend to assume that all the Palestinian Arabs are Muslims, a significant number are in fact Christians. Of the 600,000 Arabs living within the state of Israel, about 16% are Christians; of the 1,560,000 Arabs living in the occupied territories, about 3% are Christians; of the total population of Palestinian Arabs, Christians make up just under 10%. Many Arab Christians are the descendants of those who became Christians in the first few centuries of the Church's history. They are often offended that Christian visitors from the West seem more interested in the stones of ancient ruins than in their Arab brethren, the 'living stones' who provide a continuing Christian witness in the land today. Christian visitors should therefore try to have some contact with a local Christian community during their stay, and to learn about their problems and concerns. This can be arranged through most of the Jerusalem churches listed here.

The Christians of the Holy Land belong to four main groupings of churches; Eastern Orthodox (Greek and Russian), Oriental Orthodox (Armenians, Copts, Syrians and Ethiopians), Catholic (Maronites, Melkites and Latin Catholics) and Protestants (mostly Arab Episcopalians, the rest being chiefly Christian Brethren, Church of the Nazarene, Pentecostals and Baptists). The largest groups are the Catholics and Greek Orthodox. Some 80% of the country's Christians are Arabs.

There are also an estimated 3,000 Jewish Christians, who prefer to be known as Yehudim Meshihiim (Messianic Jews). Their indigenous churches use Hebrew and worship on Shabbat (the Jewish sabbath).

In addition to Jews, Christians and Muslims, there are about 41,000 Druze in the Holy Land. The Druze emerged as a sect of Islam in the eleventh century. There are Druze villages in Galilee and on Mount Carmel.

There are also small Samaritan communities living in Nablus and Holon, totalling 300–400. This sect adheres rigorously to the laws of Moses, and still celebrates the Passover each year on Mount Gerizim by sacrificing a lamb for each family.

JERUSALEM

To Tel Aviv

Herzl Boulevard

Yehuda Halevi

Agrippas

Jaffa Road

Bezalel

Ben Yehuda

Ben Zvi Boulevard

King George V

Dor Va-Dor Museum

Keren Hayesod

Knesset

Ruppin

Shrine of the Book

Derech Aza

Israel Museum

Gaza Road

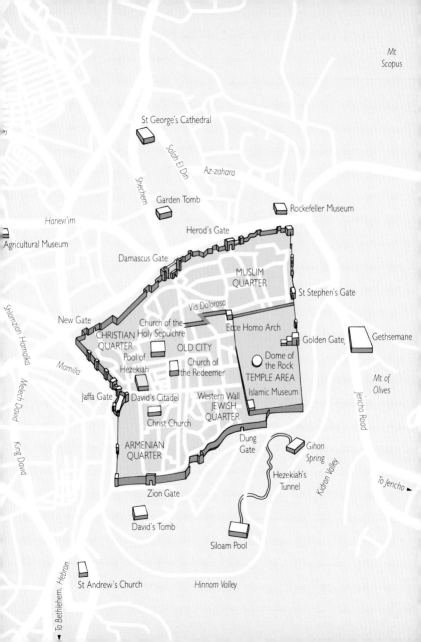

JERUSALEM CHURCHES WITH SERVICES IN ENGLISH

Full details of churches and church services, in Jerusalem and beyond, can be obtained from the Christian Information Centre at the Jaffa Gate in Jerusalem. The following is only a partial list.

Episcopal (Anglican): The Dean, St George's Cathedral, 20 Nablus Road, PO Box 19018, Jerusalem. Tel: Jerusalem 282167
The Vicar, Christ Church, PO Box 14032, Jaffa Gate, Jerusalem 91012.
Tel: Jerusalem 224584

Church of Scotland (Presbyterian): The Minister, St Andrew's Church, PO Box 14216, Jerusalem. Tel: Jerusalem 714659

Lutheran: The English-speaking Pastor, Church of the Redeemer, Muristan Road, Old City, PO Box 14076, Jerusalem. Tel: Jerusalem 282543

RELIGIOUS FESTIVALS AND PUBLIC HOLIDAYS

The dates of the Jewish festivals depend on a religious calendar based on lunar months. This means that Jewish holy days do not occur on the same date in the Gregorian calendar every year, but can fall on a range of dates within a limited period (like the Christian festival of Easter). The main Jewish holidays, with their approximate dates, are as follows:

Rosh Hashanah Jewish New Year   **September**
Yom Kippur Day of Atonement (Leviticus, chapter 16)   **September**
Sukkoth Feast of Tabernacles (Leviticus, chapter 23:34–44)
   September–October
Simchat Torah The day following the eight days of Tabernacles, celebrating the giving of the Law
Hanukka Feast of Lights (or Dedication), an eight-day celebration of the re-dedication of the Temple in 164BC (I Maccabees, chapter 4:52f.; John, chapter 10:22)   **November–December**
Purim Two-day celebration of deliverance from a massacre in the time of Esther (Esther, chapter 9)   **February–March**
Pesach Passover, the eight-day festival celebrating Israel's liberation from bondage in Egypt (Leviticus, chapter 23:5–8)   **March–April**

Information on the precise dates of public holidays should be obtained from your travel agency or hotel information desk.

Shabbat (the sabbath) begins at sunset on Friday and lasts until sunset on Saturday. Jewish shops and businesses close and most public transport comes to a standstill. To be on the safe side, visitors should not rely on any services being available after 2.00 pm on the Friday. In Orthodox Jewish quarters driving is banned, along with anything else which might be regarded as work.

Most museums and archaeological sites under Jewish control will either close or have restricted opening times for Shabbat and the major festivals (closing early on the eve of the festival). Check before planning your visit.

The Muslim holy day lasts from sunset on Thursday until sunset on Friday. Shops and businesses owned by Muslims will generally close down at 2.00 pm on Thursday and will remain closed all day Friday. Admission to Muslim sites is likely to be prohibited or restricted during that time.

Christian shops and businesses are generally closed all day Sunday, and visiting at churches and other Christian sites is prohibited or restricted.

Visitors wishing to either celebrate or avoid the major Christian festivals of Christmas and Easter should remember that not all branches of the church celebrate these at the same time. For the Orthodox Churches, 6 January is the major festival of the Christmas period, not 25 December. The date of Easter not only varies from year to year; because of the different lunar calendars in use, the Easter of the Orthodox Churches can be separated from that of the other denominations by as much as five weeks.

Text copyright © 1989 John Bimson
This edition copyright © 1989 Lion Publishing

Published by
Lion Publishing plc
Sandy Lane West, Oxford, England
ISBN 0 7459 1433 0
Lion Publishing
20 Lincoln Avenue, Elgin, Illinois 60120, USA
ISBN 0 7459 1433 0
Albatross Books Pty Ltd
PO Box 320, Sutherland, NSW 2232, Australia
ISBN 0 86760 996 6

First edition 1989
10　9　8　7　6　5　4

Acknowledgments
Scripture taken from the HOLY BIBLE, NEW INTERNATIONAL
VERSION. Copyright © 1973, 1978, 1984 by International
Bible Society. Used by permission of Hodder & Stoughton, Ltd.
All rights reserved.

Photographs by Sonia Halliday Photographs:
Sonia Halliday, pages 17, 19, 21, 22, 26–7, 28–9,
33, 34–5, 40–1, 49, 50, Jane Taylor, pages 43, 47;
Lion Publishing: David Alexander, page 53;
David Townsend, pages 15, 24, 37, 38, 44–5, 54–5,
56, 58, 60–1, 63, 64–5, 66, 68–9, 71, 72, 74–5, 76,
79, 80, 83, 84–5

Design and graphics by Tony Cantale Graphics

A catalogue record for this book is available
from the British Library

Printed in Hong Kong